Poetic
Philosophy

Brooke Dunham

POETIC PHILOSOPHY

POETIC PHILOSOPHY

DEDICATION

This anthology is dedicated to everyone who has ever been through a tough time as we know life will never be easy as that's not the way it's intended to be. Please know you are not alone and I can guarantee you that there is someone out there who will ACTIVELY listen to you. In addition to this, this anthology is also dedicated to everyone who is in my life and all those who have previously been in my life, without you all, I wouldn't have a thing to write about. Last but certainly not least, I would like to dedicate this book to the divine power of God and the heavenly Spirit World.
Thank You.

CONTENTS

ABOUT THE AUTHOR

Brooke Faye Dunham is a native of County Durham in the North East of England, United Kingdom. Growing up with a younger sister named Maddison, she had a best friend for life. At the time of composing this anthology, she is twenty-one years old. While in a strong relationship with her partner Daniel, she mothers one daughter names Amelia-Grace, whom she has with her partner. Brooke is a passionate Spiritualist and Medium and has devoted the last three years to Spiritualism, however, she has took a short break for her own well-being, thus composing this anthology. The poems that consist this book have been written in her years as a devoted Spiritualist. As part of being a Spiritual person, Brooke does not perceive herself as a "Guru" or a person of power. Humbly, she respects every living being as equal and enjoys passing on knowledge from her growth and development.

She has questioned her faith and beliefs all her life. Since a young age, Brooke has shown an interest in mediumship and Spirituality. When she was seven, her Granda passed to Spirit due to throat cancer. At the age of fourteen Brooke woke in the middle of the night to go downstairs, she noticed her kitchen door swing open by itself and a figure that very closely resembled her Granda. Frightened, she bolted upstairs, awakening the members of her family with her screaming. Later on that year, she was taking silly videos of her friend and sister. After posting the video on social media, an acquaintance pointed out a face on the side of the black wardrobe. Sheepishly, she confided in her auntie Marie – whom she looked up to like a mother. After consulting her, her auntie Marie said that the face was the face of her Granda. After turning fifteen, her auntie Marie took Brooke, her nana Ann and friends to Willington SNU Spiritualist Church and she was hooked. She attended a few other times but halted going due to taking her GCSEs at school. Her auntie Marie passed tragically when Brooke was eighteen. The whole family was shocked and broken. The month after, Brooke discovered she was pregnant. A gift from Spirit as she passionately announced. A month before she delivered her daughter, she attended Shildon SNU Spiritualist Church and fell in love with the religion again. From the age of nineteen, Brooke was now practicing and developing her mediumship. A lovely lady and fellow Spiritualist, Phyllis Eddy, encouraged Brooke to pick up the pen and start writing poetry again.

ABOUT THE BOOK

This anthology was composed as a way to help inspire and guide people through life. The poems can be taken subjectively and used to ignite thoughts and opinions within philosophy, whether it be spiritual or otherwise. Personal to Brooke, the poems have been inspired and extracted from Brooke's many life experiences, making them relatable through advanced empathy. Most of the poetry was written and thought of during meditation and/or communication from the Spirit World as guidance. After each poem, there is an explanation to why Brooke wrote them. This is to give a mindful insight. Although Brooke has given her views on the poems, they can be taken and used as anyone sees fit and relate them to your own personal experience.

PREFACE

I have always wanted to release a book. Since a young age I have shown a keen interest in literature; from writing fiction, biographies and poetry. I have always enjoyed the creative aspect of writing. Being a child who was very self aware and full of emotions, poetry was one of the main ways I could release my thoughts and feelings. In secondary school, part of our English GCSE was to dissect an unseen poem and explain what the poet was trying to achieve when writing the poem. Although stressful at times, I enjoyed doing this as it gave me an insight into the poets life and their inner monologue. After discovering Spiritualism and Spiritual writing, I combined my passion for poetry and my experiences as a Spiritualist through meditative states and thus, created this anthology. Please feel free to enjoy these poems, I hope they ignite a spark in you somewhere. So sit back, relax and experience the rollercoaster of poetry I ave prepared for you.

POEM ONE - MAM

What do I do?
When I lose you.
Who am I now?
The body that made me,
Has taken her final bow.
What do I do?

My first true love,
No where in sight.
Transcending up above,
Although you put up a great fight.

The woman who brought me,
Into this Earthly Plane,
Is now free.
Free of all hurt, discomfort and pain.

I am lost,
You have been found.
God has took you from the bitter frost,
Leaving us on the ground.

Our Mam,
Our Best Friend,
Our Shoulder To Cry On,
Our Life Giver,
Our Role Model,
Our First True Love,
Our Mam.

We hope you heal,
From all the sorrow.
We wish this wasn't real,
Mam, until tomorrow

EXPLANTATION - MAM

After the sudden passing of my partner's (Daniel) nanna, as everyone else would, I was feeling intense emotions of grief, however it was different than any other death I had experienced as this was the first time a close death had happened in my life while I had Spiritual beliefs. Although she wasn't my mother, in order to process the situation the best I could, I meditated and I was placed in the shoes of her children and I begin to write away. It was a very hard position to put myself in but I feel it helped me emphasise with the family through the never-ending grieving process.

POEM TWO – MEMORIES OF THE HEART

Here in our hearts,
Here in our minds.
When we look for that missing love,
It's nowhere to find.
There's no need to look,
Just feel it right there.
To be swallowed by grief,
Is a thought I can't bare.
Time is a theif,
Spend it wisely.
Knowing our loved ones are right there,
Here in our hearts optimisely,
Here in our minds.
They haven't gone too far.
Watch your memories,
And there you will find,
Our loved ones on par.

EXPLANATION – MEMORIES OF THE HEART

Writing this to begin with, I was feeling very optimistic about the grief I endured relating to past loved ones. I had the idea set in my mind that I'd like to write a poem that could relate to many people, even if they aren't big believers on the Spiritual concept of communicating with loved ones who have passed and the truth is, the one thing that connects everyone apart from our Spirit is our memories that are stored away.

POEM THREE – I AM HURT!

I am hurt!
YOU compared me to nothingness,
YOU ruptured my future with drama,
YOU destroyed my feelings of illness,
YOU ignited my suture of trauma.

YOU hurt me!
I chose to feel and react this way,
I will never be free,
I felt not yellow, but grey,
I subconsciously broke the ability,
I just need to pray,
It is my personal responsibility.

This is me.
The feeling of hurt,
Is the way I chose it to be.
No good running through the dirt,
I am hurt

EXPLANATION – I AM HURT!

Based upon many different ordeals in my life, this poem reflects on the responsibility I take personally. In my earlier life, I always blamed other people for the way I felt. Although they had done something that wasn't the best idea at the time (from my perspective), they don't and won't have control over my feelings, thoughts and actions – all of that is down to me. It never really occurred to me that it was (subconsciously) my fault for feeling emotions until I was training to be a counsellor. I then took that knowledge into my Spiritual Journey and started acknowledging that life is 10% what happens to you and 90% how you react to it.

POEM FOUR – **REDEMPTION**

Kicked in the head,
Trampled on the ground.
I told me mother,
And she just frowned.
All I can hear is this sound,
"I'm not loved,I'm not good".
Stop before I get slammed into the mud!

I'm all alone in this world I call home,
It's time I crashed and left this poem.
One will, two will, three will, four,
Can I take this anymore?
One sign, two sign, three sign,
Fine.
It seems like it's my time to shine!

Someone once told me "You'll Never Walk Alone"
Truth be told,
I really liked that tone.
What did I do?
Followed the light!
I really knew I could do it too
There was no need to fight.
Happiness, joy, love and healing,
This is my spiritual journey,
Come along if it's appealing.
God and Spirit are the worlds attorney

EXPLANATION - REDEMPTION

Being the subject of bullying and abuse, I poured my traumatic experiences and emotions into this poem. It reflects on some true events in my life. I always felt the need to give up and often caught myself thinking and saying "what is the point?" Proving that my existence on this Earthly Planet means something as I'm here for a reason and that reason is to learn but also to teach. "You'll Never Walk Alone" means more than one thing to me. I'm a relatively decent football fan (I'm not a hooligan) and have many connections to the song by Gerry And The Pacemakers . The first reason it means a huge amount to me, is my Granda Frank, he was an avid Celtic supporter and used to sing the song to me when I was an infant; after he passed, I would hear the song play when it actually wasn't. This usually happened when I was going through some of the roughest times in my life. I now realise it was a sign from my Granda in Spirit. Secondly, I am a LFC fan due to being introduced to the team by my partner and his dad. Our house is a literal shrine dedicated to them. It is a song that reminds me that no matter what happens in life, I will never be alone, there will always be support and guidance there as God and Spirit exists.

POEM FIVE – MY BEST FRIEND

My best friend thinks she's ugly,
My best friend thinks she's fat,
My best friend thinks she's unworthy,
Worthless, come to think of that.

My best friend doesn't like how she looks,
My best friend doesn't like her tummy,
My best friend doesn't like her face,
She doesn't even know she's funny.

My best friend is a mother,
My best friend is a hand to hold,
My best friend is as strong as Luisa Madrigal,
My best friend is beautiful, truth be told.

I don't know why,
Sometimes I cry,
Knowing my best friend would rather die.

To me, she is the most beautiful person in the world.
To her daughter, she is the most beautiful person in the world.
To her parents, she is the most beautiful person in the world.
To her siblings, she is the most beautiful person in the world.
To her fiancé, she is the most beautiful person in the world.
To her family, she is the most beautiful person in the world.
To herself, she is the most ugliest person in the world.

Why?
We will never know.
She is beautiful,
We are we all.
Pick ourselves up when we fall.

EXPLANATION – MY BEST FRIEND

I wrote this poem about my best friend. However, this could be written about anyone in the world. Everyone has been subject to their own objectifications about themselves. We are our own worst enemy as society constantly tries to change how we should look and feel about ourselves. It's really hard to get out of that mindset that you are not beautiful. No one is ugly, in my humble opinion. Beauty is subjective - it's in the eye of the beholder. Everyone has different preferences and opinions on what they think "beautiful" is. Just like how Spiritualism is. Not everyone is going to have the exact same beliefs. Why should we judge ourselves on how we look when we are so much more than that? We are all beautiful (not to be confused with attractive) because we were specifically designed and made this way for a reason. With that being said, I believe it shouldn't matter what our outer shell, our vessel, our body looks like because we have a sparkling and important energy that we all posses. That's what I tried to achieve with this poem, to show that we are all beautiful.

POEM SIX – WHO ARE WE TO JUDGE?

Sitting here, in my Primark leggings,
I look at the girl sat opposite me,
Nike tracksuit, hair in a bun,
This is gonna be fun.
"She must come from a rough background",
As I sit here in my Primark leggings,
Who am I to judge?

Sitting here, in my party dress,
I look at the bride on the dance floor,
Dress two sizes too small,
This is fun for all.
"She looks frumpy in that dress",
As I sit here, in my party dress,
Who am I to judge?

Sitting here, child free,
I look at the teen across from me,
Pregnant belly, worried face,
This is a disgrace!
"She must have no respect for herself"
As I sit here, child free,
Who am I to judge?

The girl sat opposite me,
She's just fled an abusive relationship,
Now homeless.
The bride on the dance floor,
She struggles with an eating disorder,
The dress fit her last month.
The pregnant teen,
She was abused by a stranger,
Here worried look meant she was in danger.
Who are we to judge?
A book is more than just the cover,
Please think before you judge another.

EXPLANATION – WHO ARE WE TO JUDGE?

The first poem I ever wrote as a Spiritualist and arguably, my best one. I wrote this because I felt that there is so much negative judgement in the world. I will admit, I have and do judge people from time to time, however I try to remind myself that I wouldn't like it if I was in their position. That's why I wrote this poem to remind myself to hold back on the preconceived judgment as we never truly know what goes on in someone's life. It is our natural instinct to judge at first sight as we haven't quite evolved that part of ourselves from cavemen times so it is evidently hard to break the cycle but it can be achieved. Hopefully this poem will help remind others too.

POEM SEVEN – AM I WORTHY?

Looking in the mirror,
I don't like what I see.
Thinking if I left,
What would happen to me?
Dysmorphia is rife,
My body begins to cry.
Mind and body in strife,
I really need to try.
Please love me,
Howling at the moon.
Why can't I be free?
Why do I want to leave so soon?

Like a thunderclap,
Sensations of love,
Caught me in a trap.
The power from above,
Sunk into my Spirit,
Absorbed like a sponge.
I began to fear it,
However I decided to take the plunge.

Am I Worthy of all this love,
I asked the Guides above.
The answer was soon true,
As I halted feeling blue.

Spirit bounces in our bodies,
Like electricity to light.
The world is full of squaddies.
Communication is so bright,
It only takes one to ignite.

I Am Worthy!
God created me,
Their work is trustworthy,
Feel within and you will see!

EXPLANATION – AM I WORTHY?

The short answer is yes. The long answer is that poem. I often catch myself and others wondering if we are worthy. Worthy of what? Everything. Even though sometimes I don't think I am, I am worthy of everything, because I was specifically designed this way and in the divine power of God and Spirit, I am worthy. Relating to my poor mental health and previous suicidal tendencies, I often thought I wasn't worth the life I live – I wasn't worth the fresh air I breathe, like other people tend to convince themselves. This poem reminds us that we are worthy.

POEM EIGHT – WHATS THE DIFFERENCE?

What's the difference between me and you?
You are black,
I am white.
You are tall,
I am short.
You are straight,
I am not.
You like cats,
I like dogs.
You have a Spirit.
So do I.
So, what's the difference between me and you?

EXPLANATION – WHATS THE DIFFERENCE?

Short but sweet, this poem reminds us that although we have physical and material differences, we are all connected and the same because we are all part of the divine energy of Spirit.

POEM NINE – WHERE ARE YOU?

Where are you?

I'm here.

Where are you?

Right here.

Where?

Here.

Next to me?

Next to you.

I can't see you.

Can you hear me?

Yes.

Can you smell me?

Yes.

Can you sense me?

Yes.

Then I'm here.

What if I can't see, hear, smell or sense you?

I'm still there.

Where?

Right in your heart, that's where.

EXPLANATION – WHERE ARE YOU?

A conversation I often used to catch myself having. I completely trust in Spirit now. Although a lot of people have trouble comprehending that our loved ones walk beside us every day, even if we can't see, smell, hear, sense or touch them, we hold them in our hearts and minds forever.

POEM TEN – MARIE

I know you're there,
You brought be a daughter.
At first I thought this wasn't fair,
But I'm glad you brought her.

The smell of smoke ignites,
  Like you're here.
    No more fights,
      I know you're still there to steer.

        Flashes of light!
          I can't breathe!
            Like you at night,
              I can still see that wreath.

        They're never far away,
            Their spirit lives on.
              Every night, every day,
                They are not done.

              Evidence is there,
              Open your eyes and you will see.
                This "gift" isn't rare,
                    Spirits are free,
                      Marie.

EXPLANATION – MARIE

This poem is about my auntie Marie who tragically passed in 2019. As a way of dealing with the grief, I added specific evidence of how I recognise she is around me and my family. The format of the poem is to show how, when passed, the spirit ascends to a higher form of life, widely believed by Spiritualist as "The Spirit World".

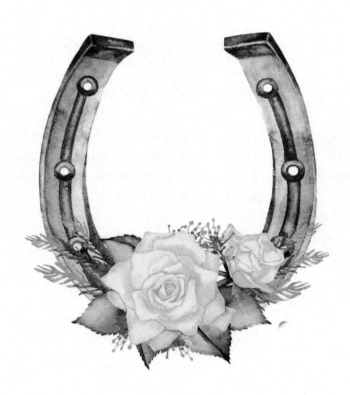

POEM ELEVEN – SUNFLOWERS

Budding and yellow,
Full of sunshine and hope.
Ripening happiness,
Standing to attention.

The grass isn't always greener,
Experience only evades.
Worrisome cheeks,
Glowing crimson.
Reflections of a sunny hope.

Faithfulness exists,
Extending the invitation.
Solitude illuminates the voyage,
Halting the carriage to a better life.
Questioning the ordeal of existence.

Calming petals brush the weakness,
Leaving only the truth of power.
Walking side-by-side, hand-in-hand,
Loneliness never knew such dismal.
For togetherness is the strongest force.

Looking at the light,
The sunflower blooms,
Stronger and stronger,
Filling the void with hope,
There is always something better waiting,
Don't worry, we'll be alright.

EXPLANATION – SUNFLOWERS

To me, sunflowers are a sign of hope. Sunflowers have a tendency to stand and face towards the sun (the light). The whole poem metaphorically reminds myself that life is full of opportunities and that if something happens in life that we don't like, we know that something brighter is on the horizon. Sunflowers are also a patron of mental health and as someone who has lived through various mental illnesses, they bring comfort and happiness to me, even just thinking about them.

POEM TWELVE – PARTNERS

You can desire love,
You can desire lust,
Your desires are a must.

Whoever you are,
Platonic or romantic,
That special someone,
Loves you,
For you.

Your father, your mother,
Your daughter, your son,
Your sister, your brother,
Your auntie, your uncle,
Your friend, your foe,
A stranger even,
Let their spirits live on,
In spite of bird song,
Eternal love, forever,
Winning.

EXPLANATION – PARTNERS

Whether it's from someone you know or not. There's something so special about feeling the love. I wanted to write a poem that would reflect how much love makes the world goes round and that love will always over shine the hate.

POEM THIRTEEN – SEVEN STAGES

Why did you die?
I was always told life ain't fair.
I say, it is if you try.

As the light shines,
The history won't ever change,
This is fine.

Like a slap to the face,
Or a strike of lightning,
This is the case.

Losing my mind,
Feeling like I want to reunite,
Leaving this road behind.

As the numbing wears,
Reality seizes to exists.
The fogginess swears.

Wallowing in self pity,
I try bargaining,
To the highest committee.

Filling with undoubtedly rage,
Why did you do it?
I'm trapped inside a cage.

The fault starts with me,
I need to be better,

EXPLANATION – SEVEN STAGES

All Spiritualists are human and experiences grief just the same as anyone else and I really wanted to capture that in this poem. There are seven stages to grief that everyone experiences at some point in their life, each verse is a stage. The format is circular, to show how the stages can happen in any order, and can repeat.

POEM FOURTEEN – **OH GOD, OH SPIRIT**

Oh God,
Oh Spirit,
When that day comes,
You can shed a tear or two,
For my body no longer exists.
I am not gone,
Nor am I far,
Closer in fact,
Like wishing upon a star.

Oh God,
Oh Spirit,
When that day comes,
Forget me not,
As long as the Earth spins.
I am not gone,
Nor am I far,
Closer in fact,
Like wishing upon a star.

Oh God,
Oh Spirit,
When that day comes,
Don't mourn my death,
But pleasure my birth.
I am not gone,
Nor am I far,
Closer in fact,
Like wishing upon a star.

Oh God,
Oh Spirit,
That day has come and gone,
For my vessel exists,
Only as a fragment of imagination.
I am not gone,
Nor am I far,
Closer in fact,
A granted wish upon a star.

EXPLANATION – OH GOD, OH SPIRIT

I always like to prepare people for when the day comes when I do pass. I'm not planning it to happen anytime soon, however, if I can do my bit in reassuring people while I'm physically able to, I hope it would make my passing a little less stressful. What I've learned while working with Spirit, is that many people who have passed, don't like people mourning their death longer than they need to, but, like loved ones to know that they aren't far apart and that communication is easy to do. It's almost like a prayer to God and Spirit for help in making the transition from Earth to Spirit easier.

POEM FIFTEEN – STRIKE THE FEAR

Lean on me,
Take a deep breath.
Strike the fear,
It's only me my dear.
Time knows no boundaries,
Yet its stood so still.
Realms beyond imagination,
Angelic, Spiritual, and Godly.
Don't be afraid,
'Tis the Earth where you dwell.
Take my hand,
Lean on me.
Rivers of tears,
Conquer the mountains.
I have brought you,
To this healing land.
Don't be afraid,
Strike the fear!
This is where you belong,
My dear.

EXPLANATION – STRIKE THE FEAR

There is a lot of fear and uncertainty surrounding the whole ordeal of Spiritualism and in life in general. As someone who originally had their doubts and preconceived ideas about death and Spirituality, I was very fearful of the unknown, but, as I've learned to trust in God and trust in Spirit, my fear of the unknown has become nonexistent.

POEM SIXTEEN – HOW TO BE RICH

To be rich,
What exactly is the definition?
My friends, it is not your net worth,
Nor how many sports cars you own,
Neither whether you possess a gold chain.
To be rich,
Is to cherish the spirit.
The spirit of love,
The spirit of happiness,
The spirit of hope,
The spirit of you.
That is how to be rich my friend.

EXPLANATION – HOW TO BE RICH

Materialistic items hold a lot of value for many people. Once over, this used to be the case for me, however, one of life's lessons is realising that although everything physically has monetary value, they should not be treasured as worshipped as they won't matter once we pass. We can't take them with us. What matters and holds sentimental value to you should be the love that you carry and the love we receive.

POEM SEVENTEEN – BREATHING

Be still.
Don't move.
Breathe it in.
Look around you.
Feel the pain.
Feel the love.
Focus on the ins and outs.
Breathing out the pain.
Breathing in the love.
Be still.

EXPLANATION – BREATHING

Sometimes we forget to live. We exist but we don't live, we
don't stop and take a moment for ourselves and appreciate
the beauty of life, no matter what we have going on.
Writing poetry gives me that time to stop, meditate and
concentrate on nothing but being in the moment. In doing
this, we can ground ourselves in order to be the best
version of ourselves we can be.

POEM EIGHTEEN – FALLING

Help!

I'm falling apart!

All of the broken pieces!

Is anyone there?

Why does everything bad happen to me?

Why me?

Hello! Is anyone there?

You're not falling apart.

Listen.

No I mean really listen.

The highest powers,

In your lonely hours,

Know exactly what is happening.

You. Are. Not. Falling. Apart.

You haven't changed.

You never will.

For this is destined to be.

You are becoming!

Becoming the best version of yourself you can possibly be!

It is written in scripture.

Leave those pieces of yourself that have fallen.

You don't need them.

They have fallen for a reason.

You are shedding the decomposed, broken pieces.

You don't need them.

In history you may have.

At present you don't.

Will you in the future?

You might.

No need to worry.

The time is here. It is now.

You are not falling apart,

You are coming together.

I believe in you,

Thank you for trusting me.

EXPLANATION – FALLING

Taking inspiration from John Roedel's passage, I was encouraged to poetically sum up the situation I am currently in. His passage really stuck out to me and I think of it often. We often like to think we are falling apart as soon as something disastrous happens, I like to believe the contrary. We are coming together and becoming the best version of ourselves we can possibly be. Things in life happen for a reason and it is all a part of our "big plan" of learning and teaching.

WHERE CAN YOU FIND ME?

If you are wanting to find any of my social media's or online presence, please see the following address, where you will find all relevant links.

https://instabio.cc/brookedunham

GRATITUDE AND ACKNOWLEDGMENT

Thank you for taking the time to purchase and read this anthology. I appreciate all of the support in anyway possible. Please feel free to use any of my poems in philosophies and other works, however please credit myself. Thank you to those who have inspired me to write these poems, without you I wouldn't have anything to write about. Thank you to my mam, dad, sister Maddison, daughter Amelia-Grace, my partner Dan and his family. An extended thank you and love to my friends, you know who you all are. Also a lot of gratitude to a great friend, Phyllis Eddy, whom told me to pick up the pen again and start writing and continue my mediumship. Last but not least, thank you to the rest of my family and friends. You all have been the light in the tunnel when I needed it the most. Thank you to all of you who have believed in me, even if your name has not been personally mentioned, just know, I was thinking of you while writing this.

Thank you all and God Bless.

POETIC PHILOSOPHY

Printed in Great Britain
by Amazon

27152515R00046